I *Explode* AND OTHER POEMS

I

Exp

AND

lode

OTHER POEMS

JACK CRAWFORD

HELIOS PRESS

NEW YORK

09 08 07 06   4 3 2 1

Published by Helios Press
An imprint of Allworth Communications, Inc.
10 East 23rd Street, New York, NY 10010

Cover and book design by Derek Bacchus
Cover photograph, 1989, courtesy of the author

ISBN: 1-58115-454-2

Library of Congress Cataloging-in-Publication Data:
    Crawford, Jack
    I explode and other poems / by Jack Crawford
        p.   cm.
    Includes index.
    ISBN 1-58115-454-2 (pbk.)
    I. Title.
    PS3603.R396I2 2006
    811'.6—dc22   2005032215

Dedication

To my daughter, KRISTIN,

who was the source of much of this work.

To my son, TAD,

for his steadfast and loving support.

To my son, JASON,

for his loving nature and the many gifts he has brought me.

And to my wife, SANDRA MACKINTOSH,

who has lifted and inspired my life.

CREDITS

POETRY
Sleepwalkers
A Breast Humming
The Wound of Innocence
Goddess of the Doorbell
Camels Pass in Smoke
Bright Flesh
There Is a Ship
The Surf Rider
Empty House
Behind the Brow
I Stand as on a Battleground

THE VIRGINIA QUARTERLY REVIEW
There Is a Stamping of Horses

THE MASSACHUSETTS REVIEW
There Is a Blue Wolf

PRAIRIE SCHOONER
Wizard Kiss

THE CAROLINA QUARTERLY
This Gaped Sucked Lung

APPALACHIA
Waking on a Mountaintop
Deer Have Been Through

BELOIT POETRY JOURNAL
The Red Tricycle
I Hear the Hocked Horse

Cont

There Is a Ship

There is a ship. Its motion moves
On unidentifiable waters. Its sea
Is silence. Its sea is color of silence.
The ship slides through color. When the sea is blue
The ship is a shadow of black. When the sea
Is twilight, the ship is a shadow of white.
When the sea is black, the ship glows.
There are no gulls, no white wings
Of shadows. No movement in the sea.
The sea is silence. The ship is soundless.
It is soundless as the white moon at night
Or the black moon in day's fierce light.
Its motion is a music of silence, as it moves
Color to color. The sea is anonymous.
No fish leap. No dolphins. It is flat.
There is no wave. There is no storm
Beyond the stillness. No sailors move
On deck. How serene it slides,
Like a moon in a black night. No cloud
Glows. No boy of the sea. Only the motion.
Is it imaginary?——the ship which passes
In the night? the ship which in the day
Passes? the ship which moves
In silent agony?

Goddess of the Doorbell

The bells of the door ring.
An instant longer shall I labor here
In these serenities.
The finger of a little girl is pressing
The doorbell, asking if I am here
In its electric voice, and hers.
It is my daughter standing in the snow.
I sit here hammering the keys of love.
A moment longer, O bright-lipped child,
Standing in the snows of time.
The idea surges with my heart,
Brilliant with colors, like the sparks
Of bursting suns, spilling rainbows.
The snow is haunted with her; the bell is still.
The silence empties me; all is dream;
Insubstantial; a drift of flakes;
The roof receives them, lifting them

Off my head; the wall holds up the roof.
I am held up by the child I love,
As surely as this roof, and by her eyes
And lips I live. A moment, and I rush
Bolt-long, heart-headed, and throw
Open the belling door to the snow.
My heart is standing there, not three;
Blonde, her lips red-dyed, her eyes
Blue as light where the flakes fall.
The goddess smiles at me, and in her smile
Enters, and light is in my hall.

Wizard Kiss

Horses yet undreamed, unborn,
Race within the viewless seed,
Trample meadows of the womb
With inexorable heel.

Radiant fish with scales of flame
Sleep unspawned;
Circlet of eye, red of rim,
Painted gills, fin and bone.

Birds that sequent through the air
Soar their necks and breasts and slide,
Unhatched, unaware,
Brood full-panoplied.

Vaunting and elastic youth,
Lounging hugged in phantom bliss
Await beyond the veils of birth
Creation's wizard kiss.

HEAVYWEIGHT

I go to greet Death as a poet.
I never wanted to be anything else really except,
Of course, Heavyweight Champion of the World!
I would have been Heavyweight Champion,
Of course, except I didn't gain enough weight.

I'm just a skinny guy, a
Thin poet. I only want to say
What wants. I hate, like Henry,
Literature. I, too,
Would drink a bowl of soup

Looking at the moon, would hear
The valved voices. Let Holden
Catch children from the cliff.
Good! I'd smooth
The wrinkles of old women, caress them

Into silken rivers. I'd
Leave them smiling in windows
And doorways, like smug fish, the sweet
Plump caterpillar just swallowed.
I'd walk with old men beside the murmur

Of rivers. My arms are around their necks.
They may have gone unwashed all winter.
I disperse myself among Eskimos.
I'd have done all I could to save
Virginia Woolf. If she *had* to do it

CHAMPION

I'd have been
The stone in her pocket. I'd have been
The cool Ouse. I'd have been
The leg walking her in—the nostrils
Caught in the snuffling strangle.

I'm only a thin poet thinking out loud.
Softly. Playing
His delicate game. Amused, perplexed.
Wanting every man's hand in mine. Wanting
Every woman in the same house with me. Wanting

All the Daedalian childers
In my apple tree. Wanting all the apple blossoms
Falling into me—as if I weren't there.
As if my foot never stepped, nor nostrils sniffed.
If you'll excuse me now, I'll go

To save a small animal. I'm only
Breathing in words. It's nothing much. I only
Walk down the street of me—as easy
As whistling, shadowboxing as if I were
Heavyweight Champion of the World.

The wound of innocence

Is the child frightened? I will rush
Out into the dark with my bare fists.
Has anyone threatened my small daughter?
I will stare them into insignificance;
I will destroy them with my bare eyes;
I will whip them with my tongue
Dipping it in vitriol. This innocence
Has tentacles in my heart. Its pain
Is a double wound from which my blood
Drains to whiteness. By her side
I am a lion. "You idiot!" someone cries.
My nape goes up, subsides.
I know. I am a fool.
I cannot hold the darkness from her eyes.
I cannot breathe for her, or think for her.
I cannot tell her life is only honey,
All golden summer forever, with the white
Heavens riding!
Her mother nigh with kisses,
Her father some beardless god.
Tears lie in my stomach.
I go out and break whole limbs
Of apple blossoms from my orchard,
Leaving the trees
Moaning with their wounds.

A Breast Humming

I hear far off a sound.
It is a breast humming. It moves
Through flowers to its waist.
It is asleep in time's flood.
Hummingbirds rub on velvet dyes.
Color is an ocean of sound.
A voice fades in density.
Flowers bend and winds come
With slow-drawn draughts. Summers turn.
Red suns glaze their discs and burn.
I hear far off a sound
Like moving grain; like smoke
Its whisper; I have lain
With the humming breast;
Been comforted; been dandled by knees,
Earth's bounding thighs.
A voice like the whisper of pearls
Crosses the worlds.
The turfy sound of pulsing hooves
Muffles at the pillowed eaves.
Hugged by the humming sun I turn,
Tugged by the blood of the moon.
Horses walk by the rose of the sea,
Proud, shadowless. They dream,
Too far for sound.
Liquid as silk, they gaze
Toward dark where no suns blaze,
Elegant, enchanted, black,
Their eyes like elegies.

Sally

Where are you I knew a thousand years ago?
Sally, with your large dumb smile? With your
Funny way of talking:
Quick and bubbly—your big teeth bared? Each
Statement ending in a burst of laughter?
Where are you who would never marry?
Some whispered you were strange. You were. Storks
Sailed over. Coals blazed. The house
Was your province, the kitchen your special place.
Hot ovens. Dashing trays of dough
In—snatching them out. Banging
Pans. Beatific. Your face
Hot and red. Taking out the garbage swill.
Pouring it into pig troughs. Calling
Soooeee! Soooeee!

Sally, they tell me you are dead, that
You died years ago. Forgive me. I
Have been away. I didn't realize. I
Would have left my yacht in a flat sea. I
Would have parachuted into your backyard, calling
Before I hit the ground: Sally! Sally! I
Would have gone out every day with you to the troughs,
Would have carried your buckets of slop. I
Would have sat all day in the kitchen
Watching you—your hot red face.
Your laughter opened heaven. No formula. No
Homily. Your altar was the heart, your fire
Roaring in it, your tongue glittering, surging.

Sally, a submarine, miles deep,
Couldn't have held me!
I'd have been at your door, soaked with brine,
Calling your name. I'd have taken
The buckets from your hands. We'd have gone
To see the horses. There'd have been
Cows chewing perfect as the curve of God.
For me you are peculiarly alive.
I hear you banging in the kitchen, your face
Hot and red.
Your lips hasten in the dusk to assure me
That what I thought was your meaning, was.

Empty House

The house is still, empty as a ghost.
My daughters just went out into the snow,
New with a great softness falling
From soundless heavens, smoothing down the earth.
The fields are full; the yards, roads as far
As eye can see; the house gapes emptily.
The voices of the girls just now
Filtered through floors and walls:
Bright-voiced talk full of colors,
Like a brilliant scarf around my throat
Shining and soft with sound.
The snow falls among their smiling lips,
Clinging to hoods and shoulders, and slipping.
Their eyes glitter in the softness, the flakes
Drifting like sleep, their gestures
Marvelous through the silence.

The house is still and I know,
Resonantly, how silence murders sound,
Throttling it with a noose of snow
Where my brilliant daughters play,
Leaving in the colors of their wake
A need for them as open as this door.

There Is a Blue Wolf

There is a blue wolf. In a lace of forest
White with ice. There are blue wolves
Loping. The ice on the trees is fixed music.
The sound is wolves. They moan among
Ice boughs. It is cold. Blue
Fracture. The slightest wind creaks. Cracks
Sound. The forests groan and splinter. Blue wolves
Stand beneath the trees. Their paws
Must be cold. Their eyes must rage in their smoulder.
The dome of twilight moans with the long sounds
    of blue wolves.
Standing beside a window in a warm room dreaming
Of blue wolves in ice forests, a dog
Passed in the silence of the street. Passed across
Four glass panes, curtained with net.
Passed with its paws on hard snow. Passed
Out of my brain and out of me through blue doors.
I could hear it down the distance. Beyond
Ice forests. In a blue glimmer of children.
A drayhorse stood hoof-deep in golden dust.
There is a coffin. They thought
It might be better if he looked. He might regret.
The candles burned in her bedroom. She lay.
He did not know how they picked her dress—whose
Fingers whispered among the coathangers.
Standing beside a window in a warm room dreaming
Of blue wolves in ice forests, a dog
Passed in the silence of the street. Passed across
Four glass panes, curtained with net.

BRUSHING AWAY GNATS

I just had a bowl of cornflakes with a
Banana sliced over it. Good, good, and the milk
Cool going down the throat on a hot night.
Remembering in a pool hall years ago
The clicking of the balls, the lampshade
Over each green table, the leather pockets.

Those pockets! The soft commotion
Of men, their sliding shoes. The positions
They assume to make their shots. The cue
Stick, smooth, thicker at one end, tapering
Good to feel, good to slide over the pronged fingers.
How they cranked the tip with chalk as if

It were one of the great pleasures, fingers
Grinding it on as if it would hold the stick
Steady, as if the ball wouldn't slip.
And the cue ball riding over the green baize
And the click of collision. And Harlan—and David.
Were you really there, Harlan, and did you

Marry Claudia? And did you not write for the morning daily
How the ball game went that afternoon and how
People sitting in the bleachers had to
Brush away gnats? What a touch!
When the riot broke at the penitentiary
You, David, got the assignment. What a

Whirl! What a going out of the office! What
A thing to be doing: covering the great riot!
Going out—all of us watching.
And when you returned, dashing in
As if you'd stopped the presses. What a
Thing it was. With that smashed hat you wore,

Your sharp face, those dark, burning eyes.
And snatching the notes out of your pockets,
Dashing off your jacket, snaring it
On the back of your chair, taking your seat
Before the machine, staring at your papers.
I can feel your concentration—you there

Sitting before it: the whole thing,
Bringing it all together: the riot, the pleas, the blood.
Your quotes from the warden, et cetera. And how
To find the lead! I feel your head working.
How you shaped your lead, David,
I can't remember. I'm sure it was good,

Full of your dash and intensity as you dragged it
Nine times round the Trojan walls and smashed it
Shield on shield and left it ringing.
The pool hall murmurs with voices, the soft
Commotion of men, their sliding shoes,
Pronged fingers propped for the pool stick.

The Surf Rider

O the gull of the boy coming on the wings of his arms
In the bare hush of the bracken wind, and the glistening
Wave rushing. His board is banter on the bells of curved
Crests. How drives the sea this boy's
Splendid car! His body delicate as gull.
Poised in stance, pressing gently his feet,
Shooting the wave's flare in foaming whisper.
Delicate as a moment. Delicate as gull wing. Dripping
Sea-god. Locks curled, greek. Throat
Lifting wide on wave of motion. Arms
Delicate as balance, exquisite as bird breast his body.

O boy of the board, plunging, crisscrossing on whispers,
Swift to float his moment on.
Rider, hold in your delicacy the perilous balance!
Foam hissed whisper. Hold in the peril of the white
Rump you ride. The horse of board on which your feet
Banter. Slapping flat. And then the stinging drop.
O curling crest. Hasten on the speeding hung
Hill of fury, foaming. Delicate, delicate!
Do not lose that fingertip of balance. There lie below
Brute bones of rock and war, bones the Sirens hurled
From bloody lips to heaps. Do not lose that fine,
That intricate balance, in rude foam sucked, spun.

Stay on the speeding whisper——aloft the breathless curl.
Swerve past sunken hulls, past heads
Drowning among centuries. Broken breasts.
Fires, crucifixions, wars, beasts,
Flicker of short swords, hurled hiss of spears.

Muffled, hugged grunts. Crossbow's shiver—hard struck,
Throat, chest—quivering, the body thick,
Unamazed. The quick
Cough of bullet. Panoplies of armor on wheel and tread.
Wheatfields of people reaped—documented.
Photographs of pits of naked bodies—heads
Aswiveled, agog. And what was girl and lad.

O do not remember the film of the women reaching
    shrieks of hands,
Faces ecstatic, to the bedside of his manner: heeled, hipped,
Twitched, fierce of medal and mediocrity.
Pasted hair, mustache. O gull of man
Coming on the wings of his arms. Delicate as lung.
Time among.
Where if the treadle of his foot miscue,
The board, dandled on tumult,
In furious glide,
May twist, careening, too wide—
Toppling. Taut gull,
Lean against the fall!

Breathed, battered, he brings the board to balance!
In a stinging drench. The white sun rides aloft.
The burnished rider, choked on crests.
Trailing his timeless whisper—
Plumed matrix—
The wave soars, unyielding, in ceaseless change,
Under the delicate dance,
Under the bantering board.

The Red Tricycle

Runs the child headlong to ride. The red
Tricycle: three wheels; spokes
Of glitters; rings of shine; silver, red;
Curve of arms, white chrome; grips of rubber
At the handle ends. Its stillness hums.
It waits; it is not restless; its patience
Is ancient. Its pedals provoke.
Eyes glisten to see its shine, its cycles,
Its red circles of rims.
Who can stay the foot? Who can hold
Back from the wind? Who can tear
Arms from their sockets? Who can clasp
This little girl, who back her down?
Who break, who stop her headlong hurl?
Children shout to see
The red tricycle. Their ecstasy
Shrieks with the plumage of birds.
The little girl is golden, her eyes are blue;
Her small face flies! Her hair is free. She flings
Her legs about the leather, and shouts,
Turning her bright head back. The red
Rims spin; shadows flash; the wheels
Moving with a marvelous velocity.

Sleepwalkers

The day: it is gauze, it is gold!
Summer in the grain, in the bird
Blazing. Flowers unfold,
Fasten their feud in the blood, the word.
Roses of amorous; dust in the flame,
Sleepers we came.

Sleepers we woke
In a world of haze golden with gauze
Girdling with glamor. Acorns from oak
Whispered in fall, fell with their laws
Into the forests. Dreamers we stirred
Unfolded and strode.

Thick is the dream,
Brooder of walls, shadows of gold
Glowing. Fish in the stream,
Dove in its glide, breast marvel and bold.
Dark is the dream; sleepwalkers we rise
From the sources of eyes.

Years in their black
Curve bitter bright back.
Summer's barge on gay
Enchanted tide
Half-dreaming slides
River-down-descending heads
Toward Camelots of the dead.

I Explode

I explode! Fragments of me go in several directions.
I am stood before a wall to be shot. In a shock of sun.
I hear the bullets coming. Bees caress a weed
With small flowers. Before the bullets came I heard
The bees. I can only chuckle. It's bizarre.
I catch the bullets in my teeth. I fire a mortar.

The shell lobs lazily. Suddenly, I'm the man
It's falling on: the enemy. My uniform is different.
I couldn't care, as it comes down, less.
I'm swimming in a great race. The man
In the next lane has my arms. They swim for him.
It's a strange feeling—one's arms

Working for another. The legless beggar
Removes my legs— squatting
In a doorway. He can't help it.
Or I sing in the mouth of the blind man
Beneath the marquee. He rattles my tin cup
I dropped a nickel in. The nickel doesn't know

Whose it is. In a hotel room a woman waits for me.
I sit on the edge of the bed waiting for me.
My ankles are trim, my breasts tense.
I'm nervous. I loose my long brown hair,
Sitting in a shock of sun. I'm coming through the lobby.
Sitting in the shock of sun I feel myself closing

Behind elevator doors. O how merry a mix-up!
How lustful! How remarkable! How juvenile!
I go in a glitter of ant——my legs along my length
Dancing me. I fall in a puff of dead butterflies.
My red jaws bite my butterfly, tearing me. I take
My numb fuzz and drag me away.

I am a horse——racing. Suddenly, my flesh,
Rippling, is stripped. I am a skeleton
Of a horse rippling. I am dead long ago.
I have the impression I died. I take his face and tongue.
I am every dead man. I walk into a room
And am a stranger. I do not understand the windows.

The door is dislocated. The ceiling slants.
I was never here before. I was always here.
I never left. I never arrived although
On my way. The shadow throws me down.
I throw my shadow against the sun.
I hide in terror or come out shouting,

Shooting from the hips——or dragging in my red jaws
My body of a butterfly. Geese go over.
I honk them. My brain is split with lightning.
I explode! Fragments of me go in several directions.
I am stood before a wall, eyes unbandaged,
Large, shining, bloodshot. In a shock of sun.
Bees hum. I can only chuckle.

There Is a Stamping

There is a stamping of horses. It goes
Through the world to the other side. It is
Horse, the stamping of eidolon.
The sod shudders. Horse before the legs of men
Straddled and rode. Before the centaur. Before
Saddle. I hear them walking on the world
In all their colors and fleshly grace. Hooves
Shod and unshod. And without shame.
And their long, fine tails. Cart
With wheels of solid wood, drawn across
Plains. Horses Spanish. Horses Gallic in their nostrils.
Asian. Mongolian. Ribs between
The thighs of Khans. Pennants rippling. Stallions.
Warhorse in brilliant harness, nervous in the flare
Of terror. Greek horse. Trojan. Persian. All
The horses of empires. Bucephalus.

But this is not intended as history, beginning
With origins, with the small, dawn horse,
But with the stamping of these horses here
In a pasture of earth, sod racked with heavy
Hoof-hard leg-stamping as they chew.
Solemn. Swishing tails at flies, green and blue.
Twitching their bodies with muscularity.
Smelling rank. Green with manure. Flies
Settling in the corners of their giant eyes.

Hugely at the canal's end presses out
In major lumps the green stuff they graze.
The mouth must gape! It is magnificent, rude
With wonder: the way the special skin
Folds back for the green mass, to press the crude

of Horses

Stuff out. Falling in heavy lumps. I don't mean
To be facetious. Brilliantly done.
To extrude—then its supple folds
Reassuming repose. Not even Charlemagne's horse
Escaped such wonder! Nor Bucephalus, in his fame.
Nor horse of Argive Greek. Ionian. Dorian.

It is the fact of Horse I want to say
Call it Imago—Eidolon. The word is shaky
It is the wonder of Horse. I stand with them.
It's like blue. They graze with massive heads.
Their jaws work mechanically. They are like machines,
But in them is a magnitude of wonder
Unmatchable in steel, tungsten, aluminum.
A haunch—stamping the hind-hoof—rocks
The mind. Planted heavily against the sod. Horse
Is here, the amazing beast called by that name.
Adam, who named it, is hardly more
Miraculous. They share a common wonder.

I will sleep tonight with horses stamping in my dreams,
Pacing with exquisite presence in blue pastures
Endlessly in motion. Grazing, emptying,
Moving their long tails, flicking their muscles.

And ever the busy and ready fly.
In morning I shall wake from deep
Dreams of horses. They
Shall walk all day with me. Their grace,
Their incredible fact. Their long, bony face.
As much a magic in the day as in the dark of sleep.

Piazza di San Marco

I am half asleep with pigeons. They
Descend on soft breasts, breathing
Frail fires from feathers, extending
Wings, slowing, skidding in.
Their feet click flat. Their flight

Is easy, exact. From campaniles, domes,
Blue spaces, turning in circles,
Flowing. Hundreds of pigeons
In a bland azure. Galleys, Doges.
I am half asleep with wings

And warm bodies. Faces pass
Me in a dream. Muffled in distance,
Children laugh. No Persians are at the gates.
Gondolas bounce in their stalls
Tethered, curveting, rhythmic.
A sleepy day. A mosaic Pieta
Glows from a golden basilica.
Pigeons caress me like the hands
Of mothers. Sunlight haunts
The air in fragile flakes, falling

On wrist and cheek. It is the approval
Of fathers. It is the slow music
Of rhythmic gondolas rising and falling
In their tethers. It is the touch of lovers
Half asleep with pigeons and still bells.

Death Is a Black Bull

Death is a black bull.

Be the matador whatever he will,

O be the matador so golden a man,

It is a bull he cannot kill.

I WILL OPEN ALL

I will open all the closets! I will
Pull the house out on me! I will
Begin! I will remember! I will turn knobs,
Smooth in the palm, go through doors into rooms
And farther doors into farther rooms. I will mount
Stairs and enter rooms and farther stairs
Into farther rooms. I will begin in the room
Of the cook-stove——in memory of Prometheus.

Out of a raw ancestry. I will remember ham,
Feel the handle of the pan. I will beg
Among Penelope's suitors, eat bread
In the glitter of their teeth. I will drink
Wine mixed with water by rosy hands. I will
Starve to death with ribs. I will fetch
Wild boars from the tusks of tapestries,
Go in harness on a medieval horse.

I will touch pots, pull them out, feel
Their cold sides smooth, the time it took
Men making shards, potherds sunk in bog.
I will open the closets of dishes, cups, colors.
I will set the goldfish bowl in a smooth sun.
I will arrange a pot of violets with my fingers.
I will tear off the lids of coffins. I
Will tear off the doors of closets, open cages

THE CLOSETS

And let canaries go, running after them to put
Them back. A thermometer floats
In a crock of home brew. I will bottle it.
Turning, my heel crushes the head of a mouse
Running to flee. I will open the oven, set
It afire with roasts, passing out slices
To tongues and teeth. I'll make broth for the sick,
Hot poultices, fill hot water bottles, give bits

Of broken glass to girls. I will open all the closets,
Pull the house out on me, turn smooth knobs,

Opening closets swollen with linen and towels.
I will never forget. The feel of linen is cool,
Turning warm in sleep. I will smoothe the heads
Of sleeping children. I will save tags and remnants,
Whole closets full, swollen with linen and silk.
I will go upstairs, feeling my muscles work.

I will hear the sound of the roof. I will
Draw the walls close. Trees will grow in rooms.
I will hang swings from oaks. Swallows
In barns shall skim the sun, horses pace.
I will remember ham, feel the handle
Of the pan. I will beg among Penelope's suitors,
Drink wine mixed with water by rosy hands.

Fondling Women

I don't know how to get into things enough. I can't
Pass all those people without stopping and asking
Each one who he thinks he is and what he's doing.

Or thinks he's doing and who gave him permission.
I would be crucified! I can't ask a woman
If her love is good. I can't ask a bank how its

Enormous blocks of stone feel. But it's terribly
Important! Each block must feel. All those people
Going into the movie, standing around the lobby.

I can't ask the lobby how it feels to have them.
And the girl with the nervous face holding hands
With a boy with a pimply nose. What is it?

What are your dreams, boy, streaming from you like vapors?
Invisible? No one can see? You are dive bombing?
Feeling the blue slip of your stream? You

Are getting rid of your pimples
And becoming an important man? You are wearing
Boots, the air slipping easy from your swagger?

You are fondling women? Choosing the one of your choice?
And you, pale girl, with your narrow nervous look?
I will step up to you. I must know what it is

You want! I am very gentle. I lift her chin until
Her eyes look into mine. But suddenly, I cannot
Ask her. I brush my tears away. But she

Has turned in, taking me shyly. She will
Never be the same. I cannot pass all these
People by. And dogs and birds. I will never

Face myself if I cannot
Get inside the skin of questions. I cannot
Go to books to get the soft reflected look

Or the feel of the block of the bank's enormous stone.

Three Deer

Doe first, followed by two fawns, one

Behind the other. Alert as light,

They wander slowly, heads perched to hear

The least-bent blade. Trees

Release them into open lawn,

Spirits slenderly supported, eyes

Luminous with seeing, ears pricked

To whispers of invisible spheres.

Grass hardly knows they're there, feels

But faintly the pressure of hooves. The doe

Pauses, head lifting, the fawns, mirroring,

Pause, heads lifting. They proceed

In a strange, unearthly way,

Visitors from another world, emerging

From the shade of trees, light

Receiving them as if they, too, were light.

THIS GAPED SUCKED LUNG

This gaped sucked lung might any lung have been,
This fish been form of animal and fur,
Or swum the sleep of darkness as the whale
Or been a woman rather than a man,
Or been the color black or the color red,
Been Assyrian, been Jew in Babylon,
Been the Man himself on Calvary,
Been the dove sweeping past his face.

I am a bellowsed blower, sucker of air,
A whimsicality, a shape of form
Who might have crawled blind as a muddy worm
Or swum in salt or from the olives flown,
Who might have been the traitor with his kiss,
Or the giant falling struck by David's stone.

POET IN THE

The poet in the cloth of himself. Curious,
His stillness as he eases into motion——
Clytemnestra's sentinel

Watching across a midnight sea.
The poet easy with his murder, sharpening
Axes or tense as edge. Or drowsy.

Sprigs, sprays, pot plants, vague windows, light,
Silence. Silence moving into sound. A wall, a roof
Creaking. Or a twig outside. Or sound

Of dog-bark, yard bitten——then still.
And bird. The mind is a cage of yellow canaries!
Vague shapes, probings.

Into sensitive areas. Sallies. Sorties.
Horsemen emerging from desert fortresses.
Blazing sun——every sand a burning grain.

Camels loping——glimmering on horizons.
A drop of dew crashing. A twitch of buttocks
From sitting still. Out of corners of eyes bits

Of debris. White oblong pad. Sense of sound.
Stool, chair, book. Its pages pressed, bound.
A delicate reconnaissance. A probe.

CLOTH OF HIMSELF

A fish on fire, a blazing bird.
Machine guns chattering in the Argonne.
A dead horse in a tree — blown there

In World War One.
Dylan, sea-rocked, says a poem
Must be knocked in the head. A good

Say! Something to keep in mind. The poet
In the cloth of himself. Behind screens.
A hawk at windowsill — poet his sparrow.

Poet a hawk eyeing the sparrow of him.
Poet poised in his skin.
Deftly, delicately.

A shriek of wheels.
Plumed locomotives — plunging steel.
But the room is still, the book breathless.

The oblong, the white pad, sprig, spray.
Silence moving into sound. Curtains fixed.
Poem deathless.

"Good Day" to Killers

Suddenly, trapped!—helpless! There, your destiny
Before you, in a twinkling. Up
To your eyes. The mugger, the madman.
A great bridge swagging, staggering: your car
Swerving—plunging off. Breathless!
It's enough to crack the brain. A
Child beside you? Two? A wife?

The agony! And there you are!
In it. Floating down from what had been
A ride in a smooth machine,
Water a hundred feet below. Your mind
Had been somewhere else the moment
It happened. You felt the shudder,
Noted the weaving structure, the lanes
Twisting, ripping. As you shot off it.

Or suddenly, in a dark street, coming
From your girl, sunk in dream, in a
Sluggish ecstasy, shadows move and men
Have you, snarling, by the throat, knives
Glinting. Hissing. Wanting your blood, who'd been
Whistling, walking with a lilt. Ha!
There it is! Your skin. Theretofore
Seamless. The knife looses you. You lie
In your sticky stuff, losing the light of your eye.

Or you happen to be passing
When a bomb goes off.
You were on your way to lunch,
Smiling with that peculiar charm you have.
Suddenly, a blast! Glass shivering.
Your smile entirely anachronistic.
Half your face. When all had seemed so well.
Trapped! Or driving on ice,
Sliding helplessly with a glittering grace.

Or a plane at thirty thousand feet
Plunging toward earth. Something to think about!
Surely, you will lay aside your magazine
As you go down, having other things to contemplate.
Teeth clenched——nothing to say.

As the car sinks in the river after plunging
From the bridge, lifting a towering fountain
Noted by a number of gulls,
You open the door to see what you can do about it.
You're not a bad swimmer. You have a chance.
But in the bulging of your heart, lungs
Blowing into balloons, you know you'll not
Make it. A slow descent. Your legs grow limp.
You got the jacket off, but the shoes. . . .
The shock! You're done. All
Is water, the dream of it. You're gone.   »

"GOOD DAY" TO KILLERS (*continued*)

In school your daughter is drawing in crayon
Or the knife has entered you, who'd been

With your woman. You're mentioned: page three.
The last thing you remember was feeling weak.
And so it goes. The chance of it. Thus,
Trapped! Suddenly, there, your destiny!
The crown rolls off your head. Your head
Rolls off your neck. Sir Thomas More,
Kneeling at the guillotine, lifts his beard aside.
It isn't the *beard* has offended the king, he says.

And so, with gallantry, make the most,
Bold, even reckless, ready for the worst.
Galahad, Jiminy Cricket, Pinocchio.
Close your eyes as you sink to drown.
Plunging from air, finish the article.
Bleeding to die, wish "Good day" to killers.

I Stand as on a Battleground

I stand as on a battleground I dreamed.

The air is thick with death.

The final man takes his breath.

Who stands in the gaudy dying, holding

The crucial weapon? What is his skin?

What is the color of the death of him?

Whose skin is sheathed? What damascene?

Whose red essence in this black mold?

What is the skin of the hand that holds?

Who is the heart that bleeds its color?

Whose is the blood that springs in flower?

Whose flower won? Whose red flower?

ALWAYS THE DOLPHINS

My daughter, studying this year in Spain,
Tells me she's staying with a certain
Dona Sanz. The home
Is two or three hundred years old. A
Marble staircase rises from the first
To the second floor. Up this she goes
To her room, ceilings
Fifteen feet high! French doors,
Almost to the ceilings, opening out
Onto a balcony from which she has a view
Of red-tiled roofs. Below, a courtyard.
Birds sing. I think of her.

Entering the front door. I smile
At Dona Sanz. My shoes click up
The marble steps. Her room is simply furnished.
Spartan. Like yours, Daddy! Her letters
Come excited. She has good teachers at the *instituto*.
One is eighty-three. If you saw him
On the street you might
Call an ambulance. He teaches a class
In Don Quixote. In class his age
Drops away. He becomes a tiger,
Leaping about to illustrate a point—
A tiger for Cervantes and Quixote.
Brilliant, she writes. I believe it.
Every word! Daughter there
In fabulous Spain. My tall, blonde daughter.

Is it true that Spanish men
Go for blondes? True in Mexico.

Leaping Before

I've written to her, cautioning,
Fearful of machismo. Ha!
Absurd progenitor! Assuming
Timidly his auctorial rights in her!
Ghost of Polonius, dealing caveats!
Deaf upon the wind. O windy man.
Wanting for her whole argosies
Of the world, wanting for her
The suns and moons. Who wanted for her
Always the dolphins leaping before her.
Who writes a private poem to tell her so.

In her dear ship she glides, her spine
A mast on which her spirit blows. Who is
My flesh, but all men's. Eve's. All
The more mine for having loved her
And been shaped by her, and been a part
Of her shaping. O so lovely shaped
Daughter! Your sails of spirit
Draw you, tall and slender. For me
You glide Madrid! Your tale of the bankers
Moves me to laughter! How they came out
To greet you—sorry your father's check
Had not arrived. Cheering you, five of them!
Banco Espanol! Who came from their partitions
To pay their regrets, ordering
Pastries and coffee, chatting with you.
How could I be annoyed, you write to me,
With such charming gentlemen! How
Could you, indeed! I am a pleased father.   »

ALWAYS THE DOLPHINS LEAPING BEFORE (*continued*)

You stand in Spain, I here. Colors
On a map. Just as well
It be Spain, if you love it, as you do. Deep
Into Hispanic history, culture, art,
Walking among the Romans and the Moors.
Live with fiery gentleness, my dear! Live
With ardor. Polonius,
Old fool, be at it now, telling her
How to do it. Live this way! Live
That way! Nothing matters but that the ship
Of you glide the dear life. You are here.
I brought you, in my way, with help of other.
I cannot save you from hurt, but think
That those who brought you here, creative vicars,
Brought you this long journey, long as all,
Out of the essence of whatever is,
Nurtured you with ancient tenderness,
Wanting for you always the dolphins
Leaping before you in the marvelous seas.
Wanting for you
All the argosies of this world. Daughter,
Sailing there — your spine a mast
On which your spirit blows.

Behind the Brow

I know that even as I sit and write

In a storm of nervous light,

Some neighbor, or Ganges man,

Resident of junk, or Cypriot,

Is red with rage.

How do I mean then?

What is my complexity, my weight?

I see dead men lie. One or two

With beards. Photographs show

Eyes shut and blood. Behind the brow

Is the brain each had. The flower

Of wife, of child. The thought still there

In the black brain with the brim pulled down.

What mean the keys under my fingers I hit

In a nervous storm of light?

Lines, Years Later, to His Son

There's something I want to say to you,
If I can, something out of the shifts and turns,
The bends of the way, the ups and downs,
The strange happenings, the vistas of being
And non-being, whence, out of the past, we rise

Before ourselves, gazing about, spelling
Our names with the letters in our laps.
You, yours, I mine. Conjoined
In a chord of being. Innocence
Wrenched from its sockets.

An open doorway, a window
Listening to a stream. Sunlight,
Day by day, in those curious times, the child
Lost in crevasses of sundered parentage,
Fatherless among the lightning.

Remember the bubbling brook, the green woods
Back of the house? The little fishes, lurking
Behind big stones, water sliding, gurgling over,
And the crawfish darting backward in the mud?
And walking together in the green wood?

And Knights of the Round Table? Lancelot?
"Yield, Sir Turquin!" Turquin,
Beaten down in a battle of great swords,
One knee on the ground? And Galahad?
And Excalibur? And horses and castles?

Although much absent in your life,
The sun and stars have kept us
Beneath a common roof. I want to say,
That, present or absent, for better or worse,
I've loved you all the way.

A Wee Man-child

for Christopher

From mountainside I gaze
Into valleys below—glimpse the glisten
Of distant water.
In my lap a newborn infant,
Weight hardly felt,
Head in crook of arm, eyes
Closed in sleep, face so small
I cover it, length and breadth, with single palm.

For the father of the father whose son this is
Generations pass in masquerade.
Eyes fixed on infant's face,
My own face slides
Back and back toward infancy,
Whisper of voices, living and dead—
Cords cut: my son's, my own.

His forehead puckers into scowl,
Relaxing to smoothness. Smile
Forms, fades. Nor scowl, nor smile.
Gas, perchance, tiny bubble
Moving toward burp.

His mother, rocking near, his father
Bending over the baby on my lap.
The father's mother
Leaning delightedly forward.
Dreamily, I glide among the moons
Of undiscovered planets.

I take his tiny foot in palm,
So tender it seems to melt.
Wee toes to play, in time,
The piggy game. Gentle, gentle.
Tuck about his throat the soft material.

Disoriented, I hold
This flesh of flesh, long descended.
Walls dissolve, ages unfold
Before my eyes, oceans rolling
Onto unrememberable shores.
I cannot find the beginning. My fingers
Slip into crevices.

I hold upon my lap
A wee man-child, deeply adored—
Newcomer to humanity's
Long, miraculous journey.

Hey, Christopher

Hey, Christopher, where are you going,
Running in little shrieks of irrepressible laughter
Down the long hall in grandma's house,
Granddad close behind, making fierce noises,
Pretending he is some kind of awful monster
Who loves you so much that, if he can catch you,
He will eat you alive, or some such silly thing.

Your little back is flying toward where
Grandma's sitting in the living room as if she
Will protect you from the chasing, terrible thing
Breathing noises and fire. Well, great fun,
My dear grandchild—and what a grand child
You are, scattering before me as I attack
With teeth of love to eat you up.
Whatever it may seem, it's very simple.
Love is the secret of it all. And this
I say to you, dear Christopher,
Bringing to you, in my arms, all my love,
As I chase you down the corridor in Grandma's
Beautiful house on the top of a mountain:
Happy birthday to you, on this,
Your third anniversary on the turning earth.

LODESTAR OF A SINGING SOUL

I would, for a moment, abandon words,
The breath I breathe: rhymed
Or unrhymed, free or scannable,
Plainspun or elegant, measurable
In breath or feet. I leave them behind,
Slamming the door——locking it.

I have escaped!——untrammeled
By metaphor or trope. But, alas!
Words come trooping after me,
Whirling insistently, pests
Whining in my ears, limning the heavens,
Fearful lest I miss the glory,
Clothing the green surround
In verbal second-hand.
Spilling from pockets as I go.

They traipse after me, swarming,
Relentless. So I say, knowing well
I am but briefly weary, unable long
To languish in a realm of wordlessness,
Lonely, needing soon to return
To the lodestar of a singing soul.

I Am Terribly Helpless

I am terribly helpless. I see someone else
And am myself no more. Leave my skin
Hanging on a rack of bones they say are mine.
Devilish! I can't mind my own business.
It's damnable how it works. They say of me:

He's not there now. And I'm not.
My crossed leg hanging in amazement. If
I smile, it's an accursed thing! I mock myself
Watching me smile. Or sucking my tooth.
Or winking. Scowling. Wondering how

It happened. What makes the lid come down
To wink an eye? What muscles and how small,
Pinned to what bone, pull the dimple round?
Or tighten the brows between the eyes. And what
Are eyebrows planted in? In what anatomy?

Or a book on a table. It makes me
Come in. I am flat. Page by page. I feel
The numbers, shape into them, like ink. Feel
The flat covers and the thing I lie on.
I smell of ink, or am the color and lie

In it. Anybody passing me on the street
Takes me with him. The thing I left, people speak to.
But it's absurd! He is a walking body.
A girl smiles and I am in her teeth. Or
A single sparkle. Feeling, I fall.

I was the spark of light—some dazzling instant.
Do not be troubled if I do not answer.
Speak to someone else. I may speak back.
Or watch my colors pass in some bird.
Or pet a dog. I may feel your hand.

Seamster Agonistes

A smooth, pearly button's

Fallen off my shirt.

Licking the end of a thread,

Twisting it tight, I squint

For the needle-hole,

Feeding it through,

Bringing the ends together

For a knot to hold it

From slipping through the weave,

Sewing the button snug and tight.

Bravo, old seamster!

Agonist of fraying threads—

D'Artagnan of needles.

DUE SOUTH

October. Leaves turn. For days,
Rains have fallen, woods drenched,
Fields soaked. River rises into flood,
Pouring splendidly, curving against its banks,
Its banks curving back affectionately.
Rain pauses to let me walk,
Scowling blackly to assure me
I'd better not linger but get my walking done
Before it changes its mind again.

Strange noises rise, far away——
Clamorous. Formations of geese—
Hundreds, thousands—passing over,
Filling the heavens, so high
They're almost out of sight
Moving in patterns of giant Vees.

Stumbling in a wet field, I keep
An eye on the heavens. Each beak's
Due south, geese in front
Breaking the barrier for those who follow.

I feel tender, vaguely sad.
The answer eludes. They sail so high,
So far, and with such purpose,
Such imperturbable clarity,
They wake in me a flash
Of ancient and mysterious longing.

MILK

Milk's a dream of memories, of myth.

Tongue white—and throat. Cows

Bend their heads to graze, gathering milk

In bags of bloated veins, dangling teats.

As child, I leaned on fences, observing how

They clamped their teeth on grass and weed,

Tearing it loose, mouthfuls hanging out,

Pulling it in as they worked their jaws,

Grinding sideways, green with slobber.

Children for thousands of years have watched

Cows grazing in their wondrous hides,

Heads down, through everlasting grass,

Turning green to white.

I see them, back and back, out of sight

Down time's long shadows—grateful

To them, who've come so far with us—

Filling their bags, swinging them

Back and forth across the world.

Until I Go to Sleep

I mount a winding staircase into air,
So high I cannot see the earth.
I don't know where I am or where it leads
The stairs sway. Am I going up or down?

Voices whisper in my ears. Far
Below, dust rising from her feet,
A child is running across a field.
A picket fence — a gate

Opens into air.
A voice, far away, calls my name.
Will someone come and play with me?
Jackstones? Mumbletypeg?

Mother, will you sing to me —
Leaving the dishes in the sink?
Holding me in your arms, will you sing to me
Until I go to sleep?

PAULINE

I was but a child, and you—
Squat, thick, your tight-wound hair
Shot with gray—
Were a distant aunt, with a cow or two,
Hogs, horses. Your chickens
Pecking
With petulant beaks. Some went
Cockadoodledoo!
And when you took the slop out
Crying soooey!—how the hogs came,
Snuffling with their snouts, rooting
In the roiled stuff,
Slurping, grunting. Magnificent!
I liked to go beside your skirts,
Your bucket slopping, to feed the hogs.

I watched you by the hour. It
Was heaven! You worked as if
Gods waited in the next room. As if
There were such purpose. As if
The energy in your fingers would weave forever.
As if the butter foaming in the churn
Were sun and moon—
Slabbing it out with a wooden spoon.
Your round face with a half smile on it.
The barn, the smell of hay.
The cows that chewed forever. The blue
And gleaming horse. The green dew.

O but how that iron stove
Sang for you!
Plying the flames with wood, the iron
Ringing. The homemade rolls you laid
In their birth dough in the tingling pan
To slide them quickly in
With a thrust of your fist in a black glove.
Sweat sprang in tiny beads
To your forehead and your lip, your face
Flushed, seraphic.
And the gorgeous jellies in their jars!
Butter yellow in the rolls' bellies.

And Uncle Miles in his presidency,
Cheeks shining as the food flew.
Miles, the proprietor
Of a country store with nails and shovels,
Buckets, bins of stuff.
What a fragrance hung there! And those nails!
Did anything ever shine so! And their sharp
Points. How they glistened, all mixed
In their barrels. The magic of it!

And the kind cow in the meadow. And the horse
Glistening. I could see it
From my window, and ran out.
Grasshoppers leaping in green terror.
How the breast of the horse shone! How it
Gleamed in the morning sun!
At the well, Pauline
Slinging the bucket down   »

PAULINE (*continued*)

The ringing of the chain—its tingling hum
A moment and the bucket splashes,
Sucks in water, her hand on the handle
Cranking the bucket up, slopping a little.
She smiles at me. I
Squat to watch some ants going
In single file, feelers out, legs
Frantic. Red. And a
Chipmunk and a purple jay.

It is a misty place, another country.
I visit it occasionally: a strange Cockaigne,
An island somewhere west of Spain.
No one lives there in the usual way.
Nor the horse, nor cow, nor that particular hay
Whose fragrance filled the rafters where sifting light
Boiled with a beautiful dust.
But it is vivid, and it had its day.
I have such tenderness for her
And Miles and the rolls
With their buttered bellies, and the ringing stove,
Pauline, with her black glove,
Thrusting in a pan of dough. Her voice
Murmurs, her spoon dips the floating butter.
The chain rings in the well. The bucket splashes.

It is a land in quaint suspension,
A curious Atlantis—sunken, muffled.
But living—alive—with a life of its own.
And hers and his and mine.

Standing on a Peak

I come to the edge of earth, and there it stops,
Oceans pouring into endlessness.
Standing on a great peak, I watch,
Floating in a rising mist. How
I'm here, I do not know.

The oceans are quiet, no birds in flight,
No fish, eels, whales, octupuses.

No one else—no voice calling
From distant peak, arms waving
To let me know. The ocean goes over
And over, smooth as glass,
In solid evenness.

I can't remember who I am,
Or if I ever was at all.
Light sinks into darkness, oceans,
Blindly obeisant, sliding eerily
Over the edge. I find
 A sheltering nook, rest my head
Upon my arm and go to sleep.

Sideshow

I don't want to lie in a grave!
My bones with my name on them
Cut in stone. Hic jacet.
To be looked at two centuries from now
By curious eyes. A girl, say. A boy.
Dragged to the antique cemetery
By concerned parents to read the worn stones
In their quaint lettering. Scoured by weathers,
Scathed by sun. Are those my bones under the headpiece?

Was it a century? Two centuries? Three?
Do they bind up my headstone with hoops of steel
To stay its crumbling? Is there any bone
Of mine still beneath the stone?
Anything? A ring of gold, mayhap,
Which speaks of woman, which tells of child
Beating up the womb like horses
Out of Ischia, as poets say,
Or a tooth or two? A filling by a dentist
Long dead, in whose chair I sat, moving my tongue
In comment on the current scene?
Suffering pain? Feeling the needle going in
To deaden me with novocaine?

Quoths the merry owl with its whoo?
Is there a hemlock, that tree
Of death, as poets construe? For me
The death-tree? Hemlock for me?
Owl hooting in the hemlock-tree?
Give me pause, an entr'acte — a chuckling time.
Break the eons. Stay momentarily

The abandon—abandonment—of sea.
Part it, as once the red water was
For armies of Israelites. Give me
A grimace of jawbone, if jawbone there be.
A dimpling of delicate laughter in the dust,
If dust there be. The dusty leavings of me:
My scraps, thighbones, knuckles, kneecaps.

I don't want to lie in a grave, my bone
Labeled with a hardy stone
Cut with lettering of some quaint century,
Among the giggling cheeks of boy and girl,
Laughing, half in fear, nervously
Impatient of the hemlock and the owl,
Wanting to be off with her jiggling curl,
Tugged by parents, their haunted eyes,
Thinking they make good case for history,
Thinking to educate the child
With gravestone, hemlock, owldom.

I see in the ground the new-laid body,
The body of me, feel
Time pass, see
My bones whiten into skeleton.
I feel silly. The whiteness of me!
The helplessness! The nakedness to any eye
Coming to brave the owl and the hemlock-tree.

I am a public spectacle at last!
The careful arrangement of my bones
By that mortician I remember well,   »

SIDESHOW (*continued*)

His hands upon my utter clamminess,
His owl-eyes peering down at me
Unruffled. With a merry whoo!
Faces passsing to and fro
To bid farewell to my slack dust,
Wondering faintly where, mayhap, had gone
The spirit in his nostril, called *ghost*,
That thing which animated his merry skeleton.

Three centuries have come and gone,
Or so. More or less. At last.
And I have come, as golden girls all must.
And the jawbone in my skull, if skull there be,
Tongueless in its laughter. And I have come to know
My helpless disarray in dust and molecule.
I'm a name upon a stone in a realm of owldom,
A flaccid clown, a petty politician of space and time.

Step right up, ladies and gentlemen!
It's free. Read my stone which marks me
Timeless as Caesar or Ramses.
Note the worn letters of my late century
Cut in stone, quaintly naming me.
Come. Do not whisper. Breathe easily
Click your tongue at time and time's mute way.
Roll your eyes as you approach some day
This dusty spectacle — who know
Nothing of me, nor of night nor day —
Nor of the universal circus — nor even
Of so little a thing as this, under heaven:
The owldom of one man's late surcease
Who is your wasted stone, your quaint sideshow.

Morning of March 8, 2002

How strange, waking, to rejoin the one
I was when I retired the night before,
Meeting again, remembering all the tags
Ribbons, buttons, shoelaces, of the world
I wake to, windows letting in the light,
A woman beside me who is my wife,
Sleeping softly in her pretty nightgown.

I wake to her, happy still,
Rising softly, not to break her sleep,
Bare feet on the floor, easing into slippers,
Rising, ankle cracking, moving
To the stairs, thinking as I descend
How I am who I am and not another,
Remembering how life passes
Little by little,

Bringing me to this place. Morning again,
Sun in the east, filling the windows
Rising as it has always risen.
Breathing, alive, getting out of bed,
I peep from a window to see
If birds are in the feeder, if
The rose-breasted grosbeak has returned.

BLUE-GREEN LIDS

Hands tense, knuckles white.
Veins. A mobile
Stirring from the ceiling, made
Of metallic fishes. Air
Fizzes in a tube, sucking,
Hooked in the mouth. A paper cup
Shot with water. A
Hiss. A
Drill whining

A storm shakes the Atlantic, sinks
A ship. I'd
Started the article in the waitingroom.
One survivor, his raft peaking
Fifty feet in air The dentist
Moves his many elbows His wife,
Petite, with blue-green lids,
Stands in the door, her lips
Moving. Two auburn locks
Curl to her scapula. Her eyes are green.

Embroidered butterflies hang on the wall.
His hands move in the mouth. The drill
Shrieks thinly, ceases. Her eyes
Seem faintly mocking. My
Knuckles tighten. A whine
Appears in her opening lips to speak.
Thin fishes stir. Later
I will finish the article. I must know.
His hands are white.

Turning to go, she flicks
Her auburn curls. My jaws
Hang wide with instruments. The last rocket
Soars into the night. Her
Movement leaves
The fishes stirring.

I HEAR THE HOCKED HORSE

I hear the hocked horse, its hooves;
Its bones under the boy; and bells
Breaking; the spell of spine; the rib-barred
Belly sides. How he rode! The boy's
Brittle belt bones; hoof-clomp; noise
Scattering chickens, their hackles,
Heads; their flaming squawks fanning past
Hacking the wind; past wagons of corn;
Past pond, small silver oval, pale
With enchanted oaks; owls;
Grassy to the water's edge the grave
Gray nag; plush hooves pressing;
And under the oaks; shades, shadows;
With hoof strokes. Boy, the hay
Was heaven! The white dust rising
In the loft flame, and the burning birds;
How they slipped their wings! Under the roof
Shafts of sun; and how
Wasps went with nipped waists;
Mud-makers; and the swallows slept.
And the small boy, sleeping and waking
Under the haystacks; suns and moons
Whitening doorways, the black night's
Domain; and the owl's hoot
Hovering; and on the water's sheen
Images of silence, and the soaring
Green
Unbreakable oaks.

bright flesh

Bright flesh! Not even the new cattails

Are so smooth. The humming of the dragonflies

Is whisper of gold. He stands beside the water.

Soon he shall swim. Birds ache with him.

Air is like color. Color is in his lung.

The sun is in his throat. The sun

Is stopped. It fixes blaze for him——and for one

Who may be waking now, in silence, yet whose song

Sounds in his blood and velvet skin.

The water blazes. Each fish swims large to him

In still music. The silence is his sound.

His foot, bare by water, stands with leaps.

And he vaults in the smiling he has found

In the arms of the woman who sleeps.

Setting Down a Friday Foot

It happened one day, about noon,
going toward my boat, I was exceedingly
surprised with the print of a man's naked
foot on the shore, which was very plain
to be seen on the sand. ——ROBINSON CRUSOE

That photograph of Mars! I
Slip into a trance. In color. To see
It. The pink, the landscape, rubble
Of it. Sweeps of it. To think: there it is!
No one's there. No little thing moves. No
Porcupine. Not even a skunk

Nothing's there. What is it
That attracts? It's like:
There it is! A whole planet! Un-
stepped on. No Crusoe. No
Friday foot. A
Whole planet! Dear God of Mars! No

Foot upon it. Vikings.
Shield. Sail. Nitrogen. How
The mind gropes. How the ear strains
To listen, the mind
Lopsided, swaying
From leg to leg. A kind

Of stupefaction. A red
Companion piece to earth. Harmonic.
A world of a place! Surreal. Magritte.
Viking digs its hand
Into red oxides. Shadows
Are there, the sun, rubble.

I wouldn't be so arrogant as to think
If I pay taxes I own a piece of the earth.
I want to be prepared——God of Mars——
To move on. Ready——
Reincarnate, Protean——
To set my Friday foot on strange stone.

Camels Pass in Smoke

I cannot see their color. Let me turn.
Take my hand. Whose is the skin I grasp?
What is my skin? Whose hand from the black
Abyss rests on my back?
Camels pass in smoke.
Men die in their skins. I cannot see
So much death. I go with whispers.
They pass me in deserts. It is black.
No moon stands. No red moon. No beast
Over the sleeping Arab. The wind…
I will find death. I will find
A bundle of bright rags. The sand blows.
The sun burns dead. How the darkness turns
Back. Or is it I turning? Is it the eye?
Is it the eye turning, turning?
On my windward left in the blind dead
Sand which chokes the wind is the red
Dead pharaoh's eye burning.
Where is the red river? Camels pass
In whispers. It is black as skin.
I hear the sounds of viewless caravans
Lost in whispers of invisible wind.
I pick my way in darkness through the sand.

Pastoral

I've never seen anything eat so slow as cows.

I think I could go to sleep

In the chewing of a green mouthful.

It's a slow dream. Cows

Hardly make a shadow. Trees are pale. There

Are no bulls. Barns are far away.

Tongues are the color of grass.

Milksacks bulge with veins.

They chew so slow I soon begin to drowse.

I've never seen anything eat so slow as cows.

OLYMPIAN FANTASIES

We sit beneath a tree, reading Dante,
Rocking on the River Styx.
Paola and Francesca whirl around.
Gnats sing, bees nuzzle,
Birds in their gloss slip and tumble,

Tingling with sound.
You, Beatrice play—to my Dante. I gaze,
Dazzled, in thirteenth century rapture.
The Po gliding, gliding . . .
We dream of towered, trecento cities,

Dante, immersed in thought,
Standing on Ponte Vecchio.
Olympian fantasies, like lightning, flicker.
Suddenly, pages trailing, ripped on thorns—
Twigs broken, opening their mouths to speak,

The forest shakes to fire, noon
Seething like a cauldron. Bushes bleeding.
A blind grazing, a gloating, a gaud of flesh,
Supple bodies beating splendidly.
We shake our shuddering sweetness, strip

The swollen ache. Tomorrow,
In the gold of our dreaming, we'll read
Plato, wander the groves of Academe.
We'll wrangle out his famous ideation
And shape the architecture of republics.

I've Just Heard

I've just heard on the radio
Of the massacre of the children.
My stomach is not comfortable,
The eggs I ate, the faces of mothers,
The empty fists of fathers.
The huddled children
Just before the bullets. The words
On the blackboard: little whispers
Down the blood drain.

I go to play tennis, the court
Squirming with dying faces, the fingers
Of children. When someone asks the score
I grow thoughtful and cannot think to say.

Pomegranate

Bracing it firmly between my palms,
I tighten fingers against its sides,
Doubling toward knees to gather strength,
Bringing it hard to bear to wrench away
Covering, seed spilling to the floor.

A royal line. As child,
I slipped through darkness to bushy boughs
Where pomegranates hung in someone's yard,
Grabbing, breaking one loose —
Tripping over heartbeats as I ran.

Fruit of Persephone,
Ceres' daughter, snatched by Pluto
To ease loneliness in the Underworld.

CHOICE

If one is listening,
Death may whisper to him in leaves
Or in the lapping of the sea,
Wave by wave coming in
With news of eternity.

In pinches and tweaks, we are reminded
(As it may please his Majesty)
That we are only guests on earth
For a period of limited duration.

Entering through the nearest wall
He stands, bizarre, in a shaft of moon,
Curtains stirring restlessly,
In subtle ways letting us know
We're short on immortality.

Animals die and do not know
Death is coming. Better so?
No. Rather an apple in Eden eaten——
Driven from innocence by flaming swords.

Deer Have Been Through

Leaving their telltale prints
In snow, stabbed
With fleet, emphatic hooves.

Alone, feet in warm shoes,
My great, soft, red–orange scarf
Wound about my throat.

Silence is breathless, cracking
Its back not to break into sound,
Hushing twigs and streams.

Deer would rather be still than move.
They have the ear for it.
I don't know anywhere

I'd rather be right now
Than in this emptiness of snow and silence—
Standing here.

Waking on a Mountaintop

A sea of fog, thick, rolling,
Covers me——valleys
Submerged——pulsing notes

Of whippoorwill
Floating from the depths.
Earliest morning's

Moist light immerses me
In silence, a freshness
At roots of things——leaves

Dripping, whippoorwill calling——
Fog, sinuous, serpentine,
Pouring over the mountaintop.

Burningly

I hear the sun walk in, go
Longingly to do my best,
Burningly, past sin or death,

Go in dream and color
With children far away,
Speak in languages I've never heard,

Grow through unknown fingers,
Drawn by tendrils
Toward suns that sink and rise,

Listening, all my days,
To naked feet
Moving beyond all rooms I know.

INDEX OF FIRST LINES

I stand as on a battleground I dreamed, *35*
Is the child frightened? I will rush, *6*
I've just heard on the radio, *69*
I've never seen anything eat so slow as cows, *67*
I was but a child, and you, *52*

I will open all the closets! I will, *24*
I would, for a moment, abandon words, *45*
Leaving their telltale prints, *72*
Milk's a dream of memories, of myth, *50*
My daughter, studying this year in Spain, *36*

O the gull of the boy coming on the wings of his arms, *14*
October. Leaves turn. For days, *49*
Runs the child headlong to ride. The red, *16*
Suddenly, trapped!——helpless! There, your destiny, *32*
That photograph of Mars! I, *64*

The bells of the door ring, *2*
The day: it is gauze, it is gold!, *17*
The house is still, empty as a ghost, *10*
The poet in the cloth of himself. Curious, *30*
There is a blue wolf. In a lace of forest, *11*

There is a ship. Its motion moves, *1*
There is a stamping of horses. It goes, *20*
There's something I want to say to you, *40*
This gaped sucked lung might any lung have been, *29*
We sit beneath a tree, reading Dante, *68*
Where are you I knew a thousand years ago?, *8*

Printed in the United States
45041LVS00001B/289-387